HOW TO DO
IT ALONE

HOW TO DO IT ALONE

The Art of Solving Merchandise and Service Problems and Navigating the Judicial System

Grace Anzalone

HOW TO DO IT ALONE
THE ART OF SOLVING MERCHANDISE AND SERVICE
PROBLEMS AND NAVIGATING THE JUDICIAL SYSTEM

iUniverse books may be ordered through booksellers or by contacting:

iUniverse
1663 Liberty Drive
Bloomington, IN 47403
www.iuniverse.com
1-800-Authors (1-800-288-4677)

ISBN: 978-1-4917-4605-9 (sc)
ISBN: 978-1-4917-4604-2 (e)

Library of Congress Control Number: 2014916405

Printed in the United States of America.

iUniverse rev. date: 10/15/2014

To my children, my relatives, and my friends who encouraged me to share my knowledge. Their confidence in my abilities encouraged me to share my methods and write this book, *How to Do It Alone.*

Contents

Introduction The Golden Rule of Negotiation ix

Chapter 1 Merchandise Problems and Disputes............................1
           Retail Chain Stores 2
           Retail Independently Owned Stores 3

Chapter 2 Buying or Leasing an Automobile 9

Chapter 3 Telephones and Cell Phones.....................................15

Chapter 4 Retail Service Stores..21
           Chain Stores 22
           Independently Owned Stores...................................23

Chapter 5 Government Agencies 26

Chapter 6 Navigating the Judicial System.................................30

Chapter 7 Small-Claims Court...33

Chapter 8 Civil Court or Superior Court...................................35

Chapter 9 The Supreme Court 38

Chapter 10 Probate Court 42

Chapter 11 Conclusion..45

Introduction

THE GOLDEN RULE OF NEGOTIATION

The Golden Rule for all consumer negotiation is "Go to the head, not to the tail."

With the proper procedures, every dispute that you encounter in life can be resolved to your satisfaction. I will explain step by step with tried and proven methods how to achieve a completely satisfactory conclusion to all your problems and disputes.

Always remember the Golden Rule of negotiation: "Go to the head, not to the tail." If you come away with only this one concept, you can navigate life's problems successfully.

In disputes concerning goods and services, the way to the top is simply going up to the "head." Start with the manager of the department and then work your way up through the manager of the entire store, the regional manager, and the CEO of the corporate headquarters. In disputes concerning independent stores, start with the manager and proceed to the owner. By going up the chain of command, you will get the result you desire. I will discuss in detail how easily each problem or dispute can be brought to a satisfactory conclusion. You will be given easy-to-follow step-by-step directions separately for each kind of problem or dispute.

Getting to the top or the "head" will sometimes involve some detective work on your part. In some cases, the name and address of the corporate offices, the president, or the CEO will not be given to you. But do not get discouraged. This information is available to everyone. It can be found by calling information on the phone, or if a computer is available, go to the company's website. Either way will get you the names of the corporate officers or the CEO, as well as the information you need to contact the executive offices. It is very important to use a name when you contact the corporation.

For problems or disputes concerning government, taxes, schools, power, and all medical facilities, I will give you other avenues to follow to solve your problems. Another method for solving such problems is to use elected officials. When an individual is voted into public office, he or she becomes what is called a "public servant." In plain terms, voters put them into office, and they work for the voters. Most of these problems can be settled easily and quickly by using their conveniently located offices. Assemblymen and councilmen all have offices that are staffed for the purpose of helping their constituents. A phone call or visit to these offices will afford you a guaranteed answer to your problem or dispute.

For many other problems or disputes, you can use the media. I will explain how to get in touch with all forms of the media. You can go to television, talk radio, and newspapers. The media have very extensive contacts in all areas that they can call upon to help you with your problems. When you cannot get to the top, the media can do it for you.

The same principles apply when negotiating the judicial system alone. If you do not have the funds to engage an attorney, normally you would give up your rights to proceed through the courts.

Only in criminal cases are you provided an attorney for free. This is known as a "pro bono" attorney. You can engage an attorney on contingency for certain situations. This means the attorney will work for you without taking a money retainer or any fees until the dispute is settled; then the attorney will take a percentage of the settlement based on a predecided agreement between you and your attorney. But there are many instances when we want justice and cannot afford to retain an attorney. I will explain how you can do this by yourself by becoming a "pro se" attorney. Simply stated, that means you are your own attorney.

There are several different courts that comprise the judicial system:

- small claims court
- civil court or superior court
- Supreme Court
- probate court, known in the state of New York as the Surrogate's Court.

I will explain step by step when and how to use these courts. I will also tell you how to proceed through each court without an attorney if you feel confident enough to do so.

Chapter 1

MERCHANDISE PROBLEMS AND DISPUTES

Retail Chain Stores

First, return to the department salesperson and relate your complaint. If you do not receive satisfaction with the salesperson, *do not* lose your temper; remain calm and never raise your voice. Simply ask the salesperson to call the department manager. When the person arrives, calmly explain your problem. If the department manager is not in, ask for his or her full name and write it down. Next, ask for the store manager. If the store manager is present and comes to you, explain your problem calmly to him or her. If the store manager is not present, again ask for the person's full name and write it down.

More than likely, the salesperson or the department manager, if present, will resolve your problem. Just knowing that you will be going up the ladder of command to the store manager will get you complete satisfaction. The department manager does not want his or her superior to know that he or she is not capable of resolving the problem.

If your problem is not resolved at this level, you must proceed to the store manager. The store manager will solve the problem 99 percent of the time only because he or she knows you are serious enough to go on to the top. If you meet the 1 percent that will not help you, proceed to the district manager. Get the full name, address, phone number, or fax number. Use any of the above methods of reaching this person.

If by any small chance your problem is still not resolved to your complete satisfaction, ask for the corporate headquarters. Ask for the address, phone number, or fax number. If unable to obtain this information from the store personnel, use Goggle search and find it for yourself. Using any of the above methods, contact the corporate headquarters. When you get in touch with the headquarters, the most important next step is to ask for the name of the CEO. Proceed with your problem to the CEO. It is most likely that you will not be able to telephone him or her. Take the time to write a short to-the-point letter explaining your problem, and then either fax it or mail it via certified mail return receipt.

By taking the time to follow these steps, you will achieve total satisfaction for your problem.

Retail Independently Owned Stores

Return to the store and relate your complaint to the salesperson. If he or she cannot help you, proceed to the manager of the store. If you do not receive a satisfactory conclusion to your problem, you must continue up to the top. In an independently owned small business, you must proceed to the owner. He or she is the person most likely to resolve your problem. If he or she won't resolve your problem to your complete satisfaction, it is time to proceed up the ladder to the top, the "head." You must get in touch with the state Department of Consumer Affairs.

You can find this office by calling information or using Google search. You will find a phone number for consumer complaints. Explain your problem to this agency. They will ask you to put your complaint in writing. When they receive your complaint, they will contact the store. They are there to serve you and will do everything possible to bring your problem to a satisfactory conclusion.

If by any chance you are still not completely satisfied, do not give up. There is still the judicial system. Proceed to the small-claims court. Phone the court and ask for the maximum amount you can sue for in this court. Each state has its own limits as to the amount you can sue for damages. If the amount you're seeking is within the jurisdiction of this court, proceed in this venue.

Get directions to this court and go down and take out a summons against the owner of the business. This is a very easy procedure to accomplish. You will be given an easy-to-fill-out form, and for a nominal fee, you will be given a court date. The court will take care of serving the summons on the business owner, and it will be up to him or her to appear in court on the hearing date. If the owner fails to appear, you will win your case automatically and obtain a money judgment against your opponent.

When you arrive at court, do not be shy. The courtroom will be full of people trying to find justice. Take a seat in the front of the room so the judge will see you while you are waiting for your case to be heard. When you are secure in the knowledge that you are right, you want to expose yourself to the judge.

When you are called to present your case to the judge, remember that the most important thing is to *never lose your temper and raise your voice.* Speak slowly and in a very low tone. Explain in detail exactly what has brought you to court. Do not become upset if you hear your opponent stating untruths. Just be honest yourself when giving the facts to the judge.

By following these instructions, you should come away from your dispute completely satisfied.

I would like to tell you a story about my personal experiences with retail chain stores so you will understand how I learned to go to the head to get a satisfactory result. My experiences are not unique, and although the places and nature of the disputes may be different, the similarities can be used in solving your own personal disputes.

Several years ago my daughter relocated to Florida. She met a young man and fell in love; within months they were engaged. She is my youngest child and only daughter. I met her fiancé and was completely taken by him myself. He was her boss, very good-looking and extremely personable. My daughter had a very dysfunctional relationship prior to meeting this young man. I had dinner with him and my oldest son, who lives in Florida. We both were very happy with him. I then invited him to dinner and had not only my son but also two of my very dear friends, whose opinions I respect highly. These friends were my mentors throughout my life. We all agreed that my daughter hit a home run with this person.

I spend my winters in Florida, so I was able to spend a lot of time with the happy couple. We discussed the wedding plans and when and where it would take place. Just before I left, he asked permission to marry my daughter and said he would give her a ring before I left for home. I returned to New York an extremely happy parent. It was a dream come true for my daughter. We started making arrangements for the wedding. They wanted to have the wedding in New York. When it came time for my daughter to select her wedding gown, she asked me to return to Florida so we could pick out the gown together.

Being a single parent, I knew I would have to work with a very tight budget to give my daughter a beautiful wedding. I found a discount bridal store with branches in practically every state. I returned to Florida, and we went to pick out my daughter's gown. It was a wonderful experience, and we had hundreds of gowns to choose from.

We were able to get everything we needed at the same store. We chose undergarments, a crinoline, her veil, and shoes.

When we proceeded to check out, I was told everything had to be paid in full at this time. It was store policy that unless the gowns were paid in full, they could not order it. I wasn't expecting such an immediate expense and was told I could open a charge account with the store and the payment would be deferred for three months. I signed all the forms and the agreement that in three months the payment would be put on my charge account.

Unfortunately my daughter's fiancé turned out to be a con artist. Thankfully we all found out in time to prevent an even greater tragedy. I was extremely upset emotionally and psychologically. It was a most upsetting time for me and my daughter. When I took control of myself, I started to go about canceling the arrangements I had made.

I contacted the bridal gown store and spoke with my salesperson. I explained I hadn't picked up the gown yet and no alterations had been made on the gown. All they had to do was put the gown back in their inventory. She was very sympathetic but said she could not refund my money. Their policy was clearly stated on the receipt, and also there were signs posted at the checkout counters and the customer service desk. I was told to take the gown and try to sell it on eBay. Although I was very upset emotionally over the hurt my daughter and I suffered, now I was to suffer a financial loss also.

It was extremely hard not to lose my temper, but I did accomplish this. I asked to speak with the store manager. She reiterated the store policy and refused to give me a refund. At this point I asked her to give me the phone number or address of the corporate offices. She was very obliging. She looked up the address and phone number for me. I left and went home.

Since I didn't have access to my computer in Florida, I called the corporate headquarters in the morning and asked for the name of the president. I was transferred to a woman from his office. She asked what the problem was about; I answered that I felt I should talk directly to the president. She very nicely asked me to explain the problem to her as she did have authority to rectify disputes and problems.

I explained my problem and told her I didn't think it was fair to me not to refund my money as I had not even picked up the gown and no alterations were made on it. I told her I felt that the policy they had was extremely harsh on people who suffered from emotional problems as well as financial ones. She was very understanding and promised to get back to me that afternoon.

In approximately three hours, my phone rang; it was the manager from the bridal shop whom I had spoken with. She told me she had heard from the corporate headquarters and would give me a refund for the wedding gown that I had paid for. Also, she said I could bring back to the store the undergarments, crinoline, veil, and shoes I had taken home for a refund on these items as well. It was very satisfying to feel I was not being taken advantage of by this store and that the money I could certainly not afford to lose was saved. It was a wonderful conclusion financially, of course, but also psychologically.

I want to tell you of another experience I had concerning merchandise. The story is entirely different, but using the same instructions, you can apply this to any situation you encounter and come away completely satisfied.

I went to a large department store that was having a very big clearance sale. Being a bargain lover, I went to see what I could find. After a considerable period of time, I found some really worthwhile items, one of which was a pair of designer golf shorts. They fit perfectly, and I was really pleased with the shorts. The only problem was that there was no ticket on the shorts. I went to the salesperson and asked how we could determine the price. She told me to bring her another pair of shorts identical to the one I had. I explained I couldn't find another pair in the department. She went to search for herself. Coming up empty-handed, she said she could not sell the shorts to me because there was no way to determine the sale price without a ticket on them.

I asked her to call the department manager. She replied that it was her day off. I asked her to call the department store manager. She put a call in for her, but her phone wasn't working. I asked where the executive offices were and explained I would go personally to see the store manager. When I arrived, I asked the receptionist to see the manager. She asked if she could help me, but I firmly told her I wanted to speak with the manager personally. The manager came out to see me very quickly, and I explained my problem. I wanted to purchase the golf shorts and didn't want to leave without them. She asked me to give her a few minutes and she would be able to help me. She asked if I wanted to continue to shop or have a seat and wait. I chose to wait as I was finished selecting my purchases.

Within less than ten minutes, she had a very attractive sale price, which I accepted happily. This was a very easy process that anyone can follow. You must not give in to anything that you feel is not correct. Why should you miss out on an item because it didn't have a price ticket on it? In retail, the customer is always right, and customer relations are a top priority for business.

Another experience I had concerned a gift for my son. Again I used the same steps to solve my problem. Many years ago when my son was approximately ten years old, he wanted a metal detector for his birthday. We lived near the ocean and spent a lot of time on the beach. He saw people using a detector on the beach, and he was very impressed with the idea of finding hidden treasure. Of course, I decided that this would be a wonderful gift for my son. I went to an electronics equipment chain store to purchase my gift.

I had many metal detectors to choose from. They all came in plastic sealed boxes, with pictures and descriptions printed on the outside of the boxes. I saw a metal detector that looked perfect for my son. It had a picture on the cover of a boy wearing a nice headset, which I felt would be perfect for my son. I purchased the item, and on his birthday, I happily presented him with this present. But when he opened the box, I was shocked to see it came with one earplug instead of the headset displayed on the cover and had many little pieces that had to be assembled. My son was terribly disappointed with the little earplug, as was I.

I explained to him that we would take the gift back to the store and exchange it for one that came with the headset and was fully assembled. When I returned the gift to the store, I was told that since I opened the cellophane wrapper on the box, I could not return the metal detector. The salesperson showed me the policy that they could not accept the return. I asked for the manager, and he restated the fact that the policy was clearly stated, and he could not accept the return. I tried in vain to explain that unless I opened the box I could not see that the product was not the same as featured on the outside of the box. I could not get any satisfaction and was forced to leave with my metal detector.

I knew that this was false advertising. How could I have known that the product was not the same as pictured on the box? I decided I would not be forced to keep this metal detector, which was not what I believed was featured on the box. I went on the Internet and found the state Department of Consumer Affairs. I explained exactly what had happened and was told that it seemed I was totally right about it being false advertising. The state employee I spoke with gave me the choice of mailing the metal detector to his office, or if I preferred, bringing it over myself. It was a local office not far from my home, so I decided that to expedite the situation I would go to the office myself. By doing this my son could get to enjoy his gift without further delay.

I arrived at the office and was greeted by a very pleasant person. I explained the problem and showed him the box. He agreed that this was a clear case of false advertising. He called the store and spoke with the manager. After a brief conversation, he instructed me to go back to the store for a refund. I expressed my nervousness as to how the manager would react when I came in for the refund. He was extremely rude when I approached him myself about the problem. The gentleman reassured me that I would be treated with respect and pleasantness when I returned to the store.

True to the word of the Department of Consumer Affairs employee, when I returned to the manager who had been so rude, I was greeted with a totally different attitude than what I had received when I originally asked for a refund. He took care of me immediately and made no comments as to what had transpired.

As you have read, a satisfactory result can easily be achieved by following the advice I have given you. There are many different problems that can arise when dealing with all types of businesses, but the bottom line is actually the same when you go to the top.

Remember to always start at the place where the problem originated. You must never attempt to go directly to the top. You must climb the ladder one rung at a time. Going directly to the top and bypassing the person where the problem began simply displays that you are not a person who is reasonable but simply want to create a problem where none exists. Many times you will achieve satisfaction before you climb to the very top. So when you go to the top one step at a time, you are viewed as a rational person since you simply did not receive help at lower levels.

Chapter 2

BUYING OR LEASING AN AUTOMOBILE

Dealing with car dealerships can be a basis for many problems and complaints. Many times when you purchase or lease a new car, it can be a very trying experience. We know exactly what we want, but often receive a car that is not what we ordered. It can be lacking certain equipment or may be a different model.

When picking up your new car or lease and the equipment or model is not what you ordered, follow these instructions to achieve a satisfactory conclusion to your dispute.

First, advise your salesperson of your dissatisfaction, explaining calmly what it is that is wrong with the car you were given. If he or she cannot help you, ask for the manager of the dealership. Again, calmly explain what is wrong with the car. If he or she refuses to satisfy you, do not get upset. Tell him or her that the explanation given to you is not acceptable. If possible, do not leave with the automobile until the issue is solved. If you must take possession of the automobile, get the information needed to pursue the problem at a later time.

Ask the manager for the name, address, and fax or phone number of the owner of the dealership. Get in touch with the owner using any of the above-mentioned methods and relate your problem to him or her. At the same time, also ask the manager for the address, phone number, and fax of the corporate headquarters of the auto manufacturer and the corporate headquarters of the specific division of the manufacturer of your car.

Get in touch with the owner of the dealership, the corporate headquarters of the auto manufacturer, and the corporate headquarters of the specific division of your car using any of the methods mentioned in this book—telephone, fax, or mail. Allow a few weeks to receive their replies to your problem. If you do not receive a satisfactory response, you must go on to the next step up the ladder, to the "*head*."

Call information for the phone number of the state Department of Consumer Affairs or use Google search. Go to or call the Department of Consumer Affairs and relay your complaint. Follow their instructions for documenting your complaint.

Next, find the phone number of the state attorney general. Contact that office and follow their instructions for reporting your complaint. Allow a few weeks to receive their reply to your request. If you still do not receive satisfaction, you must proceed to the media.

Start with talk radio. When a radio show opens its lines, call in. Compliment them on their program and proceed to ask for help with your problem. Next, call all the local news stations on your television. Each station will have a program or person designated as a "problem solver" or some similar title. Relay your problem and wait for their answer. Finally, call all the local newspapers and relate your problem; see if anyone wants to pick up the story and help you.

If you have a legitimate complaint, you will have a satisfactory conclusion using this method of going to the "head." You must not become discouraged, but must take the time to continue on up to the top of the ladder, and you will achieve a good result.

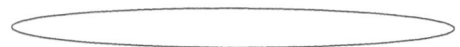

I want to share my first experience leasing an automobile by myself. I had leased my automobile three years prior and I was very pleased with the model and its features; also, financially it was within my budget. So when it was time to turn my car in, I decided I would just lease the same model for the next three years. I was comfortable going to a familiar dealer because for the first time I would be leasing an automobile by myself.

I went to the showroom and told the salesperson that I was turning in my lease and wanted to lease another automobile exactly the same as the one I was returning. I told him I wanted the same model with all the same features. He told me it would be no problem and he could get me the same model automobile with the same features. I was very pleased how easy it was to make this transaction, but I was in for a surprise.

As my automobile salesperson was writing up the new contract, I reminded him I wanted the exact same model I was returning. He reassured me again that it was the same model I was bringing back. I left the showroom feeling proud that I had accomplished this transaction alone. I felt I would be able to navigate life independently and I would be all right.

I received a call from the dealership that my lease was in, and I could come in and pick it up. Unfortunately, I had plans that day and suggested coming in the following day to pick up my automobile. My salesperson wasn't going to be in the following day and told me he would wait for me that evening, so we made an appointment to pick up my lease at eight that evening. When I arrived, he was waiting for me. The showroom was closed, and there were only myself, the salesman, and someone from the service department there that evening. I brought my automobile into the shop so the license plates could be transferred to my new lease. Then my salesman and I went into the showroom to conclude the paperwork. When all the paperwork was signed, my salesman and I returned to the shop, and there was my new lease ready to take home.

We walked around the automobile. It was all shiny and new and had my license plates on it. Then the salesman opened the door and handed me two sets of keys. I immediately realized that the keyless entry device was not with the keys. "You forgot to give me the keyless entry device," I told him. He replied that this model did not come with keyless entry. It was not the model I had just returned; it was a basic model. It was missing the many features that I had enjoyed on my previous lease. The rear seats did not fold down for a larger truck space. The side-view mirrors were not powered, there were no vanity lights, and other conveniences were missing. But the most important feature for me was that it did not have keyless entry.

I was extremely upset since this would be the first time in my life I would be traveling alone without keyless entry. The keyless entry was not only a convenience but also a safety feature. When entering my automobile at night, I would be able to open my door very quickly and enter my automobile and lock the door. I would not be able to do this if I had to fumble to find the lock, insert the key, and then open the door and enter.

My salesman's answer was that I had just signed all the papers, and this automobile was mine. I could not refuse the lease, and I had leased this particular automobile. He assured me that I could return in the morning, and something would be worked out to bring this problem to a satisfactory conclusion. There was nothing I could do tonight. I was very disappointed when I left with this new leased car. I felt this problem might not be solved and I would be driving this automobile for the next three years.

My fears and uneasiness about leaving the showroom with this automobile were confirmed when I returned the next day. The salesperson I spoke with said there was nothing he could do. He insisted that I had ordered this model. At my request, he took me to talk to the manager of the dealership. The manager reiterated that I had made the mistake. I tried in vain to explain to both of them that I had asked for the same automobile as I was returning. I asked the salesperson several times before I ordered it. I even refused a test ride because I explained I had driven this automobile for three years and enjoyed it very much, which was why I was leasing the exact same one. After a lengthy discussion, the manager made me an offer to resolve the problem. He offered to install an alarm system at dealer's cost, but I would have to keep this automobile for the duration of my three-year lease.

I'm certain many people would have accepted this offer as a solution to the problem. It is absolutely fine if you fall into this category. But if you are like me, it wasn't a good conclusion. I felt I was taken advantage of, and the dealership should not be allowed to continue this deceptive practice. I did not want any other woman who was alone like me to be taken advantage of. I told him his offer was unacceptable. I had been taken advantage of, and since he would be unable to change my lease for the model I was expecting to receive, he should pay the cost of the alarm system. After all, I would be driving an automobile that had many conveniences missing from it for the next three years. The keyless entry was the one feature I had to have. It would enable me to feel safe when traveling alone in the dark. I told him I would take this matter up with the owner of the dealership, the manufacturer of the automobile, the state Department of Consumer Affairs, and the state attorney general. His reply was, "Do what you want." He would not change his position.

At this time, as I have said before, many people would have been happy with the manager's offer. They would have negotiated a conclusion that was satisfactory for them. I, on the other hand, felt I had negotiated a deal in good faith, and it was not delivered as promised. I felt because I was alone, I was a target for deception, so I continued to the top to resolve my problem to my satisfaction.

I started my climb up the ladder by writing a letter to the owner of the dealership, with copies to the manufacturer and the division of the manufacturer. Then, using the Internet, I located the state Department of Consumer Affairs and called them. I was told to send a letter explaining my complaint against the automobile dealership. I wrote my letter and mailed it out as soon as possible. Then I called the state attorney general's office and was told a complaint form would be mailed to me. Within a few days the form arrived from the attorney general's office. I filled out the forms and sent them back immediately. At this point, there was nothing more to do except wait for the replies. I felt content that I had done everything I could possibly do to bring my problem to a satisfactory conclusion, and I always had the option to buy the alarm system.

About three weeks later, I received a letter from the attorney general's office. It explained that they had sent forms to the dealership so they could explain their side of the dispute. After receiving the dealership's explanations, the attorney general's office concluded I was right and they were going to rectify the situation. I was told to get in touch with the manager to make arrangements to have my alarm system installed. I called that same day and spoke to the manager. He was very polite and explained to me that I could pick the time and the day to have the system installed. I was very surprised and pleased that I would not have to leave my automobile at the shop; it would be taken care of while I waited. Also, I picked the day and time to have it done.

When I arrived at the dealership, the manager was waiting for me. There was a mechanic also there with the alarm system. The manager escorted me to the waiting room and offered me coffee and a bagel while I waited. Then, very politely, he asked me why I had contacted the attorney general's office with my problem. I told him honestly that it was he who told me "Do what you want" when he would not give me the alarm system. He remained polite and gave me no argument about the situation. Within thirty minutes my car was ready. He personally escorted me to my vehicle and explained everything about the alarm system.

Then the manager told me to feel free to contact him if I had any problems with my automobile. I drove the car for three years without experiencing any problems.

Chapter 3

TELEPHONES AND CELL PHONES

There are many consumer problems that can arise concerning telephones and cell phones. With cell phones, there are many plans to choose from, and they vary widely. Sometimes you accept one plan, and the same company comes out with a new plan. When you try to switch, you may not be able to. They offer certain plans to new subscribers, but not to customers who are already signed up. This is only one example of problems that arise with cell phones.

Your land telephone also can cause many problems. Problems can be very serious if they result in you losing your service. Having a working telephone in your home is not only a convenience, but also a necessity for your safety and health. We need telephones to call for medical help and our personal safety.

I will give you easy-to-follow steps to ensure any legitimate problems you encounter can be solved. You can achieve a satisfactory conclusion to your disputes.

First, you should call customer service. Calmly explain your problem. If you do not get any satisfaction, ask the customer service representative for his or her full name, and if the employee has one, his or her ID number. Then ask to speak to his or her supervisor. Again relate your problem to the supervisor. If your problem is not resolved to your full satisfaction, ask for the supervisor's full name. Then ask the supervisor for the address, phone number, or fax number of the executive offices, as well as for the name of the president or CEO of the corporation.

Using telephone, fax or mail, get in touch with the president or CEO. If your problem is not an emergency, you must wait for a reply. If your problem is urgent and is not resolved by the above methods immediately, go on to the next step up the ladder to the top.

Call information for or look up in Google search the number of the state Power Commission. They oversee electricity and telephone providers. Call and ask for help with your problem.

Also use talk radio for help. These radio hosts have a vast number of contacts in all areas, so they can get problems solved very quickly. Tune into their shows and when they open their lines to the public, call. Politely ask for help with your problem. Be sure to compliment them first. Begin by telling the host how smart and knowledgeable he or she is. Explain that you listen to him or her all the time. Tell him or her it is an emergency and you need immediate action.

Along with going to the Power Commission and radio, go to your government officials. Call information or use Google search to find your assemblyman, councilman, or senator. Cross party lines if necessary. Just go to the person in your district, whether Democrat or Republican. If you do not achieve satisfaction with one representative, try someone else.

Call the local office of the politician and tell them about your problem. Explain that you are a constituent and need help. They will usually ask you to write a letter stating your problem if there is enough time. If it is a dire emergency, they will start working for you immediately. They will *always* follow through and give you an answer as to the outcome. You elect your government officials, and they are available to serve you with your problems. They are happy to assist you with your disputes because it is a wonderful way for them to spread the word about themselves. When election time comes around, you and everyone who hears your story will be at the polls voting. They are in office because they help the constituents in their districts.

If you follow all these steps I have given you in the preceding paragraphs, you will solve your problem alone. You will have the satisfaction knowing you are capable of accomplishing this by yourself.

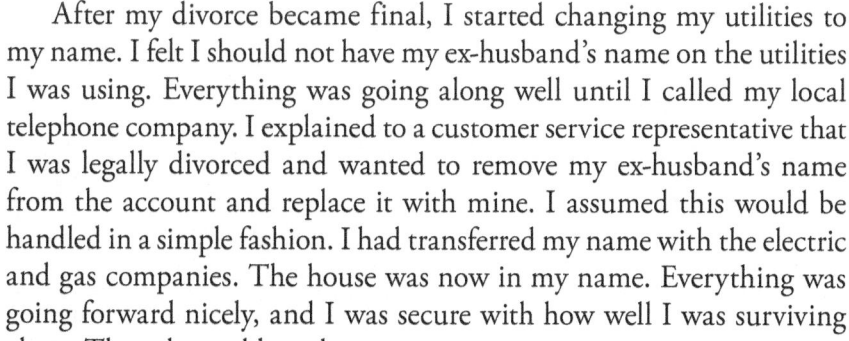

After my divorce became final, I started changing my utilities to my name. I felt I should not have my ex-husband's name on the utilities I was using. Everything was going along well until I called my local telephone company. I explained to a customer service representative that I was legally divorced and wanted to remove my ex-husband's name from the account and replace it with mine. I assumed this would be handled in a simple fashion. I had transferred my name with the electric and gas companies. The house was now in my name. Everything was going forward nicely, and I was secure with how well I was surviving alone. Then the problems began.

After looking up the account, the customer service representative told me I could not take my ex-husband off the account and put my name on it. She explained that according to the rules of the telephone company, only he could remove his name from the account. I explained that I did not know where to find him. I had no information as to his phone number or address. He was not working, so there was no business address. Finally I thought she started to listen to what I was saying. When I explained that I had use of the telephone and it would be to their benefit to put the service in my name, I was trying to be honest with them. I foolishly even explained that if he remained responsible for the payment of the bills, I would not be liable to pay for the telephone I was using.

I thought the problem with the telephone company was solved. The representative agreed that his name should be removed from the account. But my problem was just beginning. I had unknowingly opened a new can of worms. She now told me I had to submit a deposit since I was opening a new account in my name. I had forty-eight hours to do so, or my service would be discontinued. I tried in vain to explain I was just trying to do the right thing by putting the phone in my name, but she would not budge from her stand that in forty-eight hours my phone would be cut off if I did not provide the deposit. At this time I was not in a good financial position. After a four-year court battle, I was trying to get my finances in order.

I knew I would have to act quickly to keep my phone service without any interruption. I went to my phone book under government agencies, and I found the Power Commission. They regulated the phone company. I called and explained the conversation I had with the phone company and the resulting consequences. I was told they would get in touch with the phone company and try to resolve the issue within the next forty-eight hours. I was still very uneasy about the situation and decided to put a call into my assemblyman's office. I explained my problem, and they said they would see what they could do to help me. The next morning I was listening to talk radio, and when they opened their lines to the public, I called in. The host agreed that the phone company was acting completely unreasonably and that he would try to resolve my problem.

That very afternoon I received a call from the telephone company's president's office. My problem was solved. The service would continue with no interruption, and I would not have to pay a deposit for my service. I thanked him and explained I was very upset and worried that my service would be turned off. His answer was that he knew how upset I was because he received calls from the Power Commission, the assemblyman, and the radio host.

I received help by reaching out to everyone who I thought could possibly help me. Alone you do not have the power to be heard by a big corporation. But when you contact powerful individuals and the media, you will get results.

Another problem I encountered was with my cell-phone provider. I bought my first cell phone when I was alone and had to rely on myself. It became apparent that a cell phone was very good for a person who lives and travels alone. I contacted all the major cell-phone providers in my area. When I found the company that fit my needs financially, I bought my phone and signed up for their service. A two-year contract was needed to start service. This is the practice of all cell-phone companies at this time.

After I had the service for approximately three weeks, I was watching television when a commercial for my cell-phone company was shown. It had a wonderful service package. It was less than I would be paying on my contract and offered more minutes than I was receiving. I called customer service and asked if I could switch to the new contract I had heard about on the television. The representative explained to me that the plan offered was only for new customers starting service. I explained I had just purchased my phone and started service a few weeks ago; I hadn't even received my first bill. Couldn't I be considered a new customer? Her reply was "no."

Although this representative was very firm about the policy of her company, I felt this was not fair to consumers who had just recently purchased service and signed a contract in good faith. I decided I would not accept the explanation given to me by the cellular-phone's customer service representative. I was outraged and felt they were taking advantage of their customers. Not only would this cost me financially, but also I felt very badly about not making a good decision about my purchase. In my heart I really believed this policy was totally wrong. Using a policy like this would in the long run prove detrimental to the growth of the corporation.

I went to my computer and looked up the website for this cellular company. Such websites have all the information you need to find the executives and CEOs of the corporation. The names do not come up immediately on the website, but I kept looking and finally found the information I wanted. I decided by reading the details of what their job responsibilities were, whom I wanted to contact. If you don't have access to a computer, you can get this information by telephone. Then you will be able to get in touch with the corporate headquarters.

Next I proceeded to write my letter. Using the reasons I felt were justified, I started to compose my letter. I explained how I had tried to resolve this problem with their customer service representative and could not. I wrote that I realized a corporation must always strive for expansion by attracting new customers to build their consumer base. But at the same time, they should try to hold onto their old faithful customers. I explained my position that in a business that was very competitive, it was imperative to hold onto old customers as well as attract new ones.

In approximately two weeks I received a phone call from someone from the executive office. She explained they had received my letter and apologized for the inconvenience. She continued by telling me I would be able to change to the new service plan immediately. I was thanked for choosing their company, and she hoped I would continue staying with them in the future.

I have remained a loyal customer with this same company for ten years. Whenever any problems arise, they always respond in a positive manner.

Chapter 4

RETAIL SERVICE STORES

As an example of retail service stores, I will focus on dry cleaners and tailors. In terms of the problems that may arise, I will discuss clothing that has been damaged. For example, dry cleaning may result in a garment that has been shrunk, faded, or ripped. A tailor may have altered a garment, and it comes out unfit to wear. It cannot be repaired, and thus clothing has been lost. These are problems that occur quite often, and many times you are not compensated for your losses. I will now explain to you how to reach the top.

Always return to the establishment where the problem first occurred. You must climb the ladder one rung at a time. But keep in mind you will succeed if you continue to the top, the "head." Using the following easy-to-understand steps, you can solve your problems alone.

Chain Stores

First return to the establishment and explain your problem to the clerk. This person will probably not have the authority to correct your problem, but always start at the beginning. Politely ask the clerk to call the manager of the store.

Explain to the manager how your garment was ruined. Ask him or her what he or she will do to compensate you for your loss. If it is acceptable to you, your problem will be solved at this time. If you are not satisfied, you must continue going up to the "head."

Ask the manager if there is a district or regional manager. Get the manager's full name. Find out how to get in touch with him or her. Be sure to get a telephone number, fax number, or address. Using any of these methods, get in touch with this person and relate your problem to him or her. Give the names of the clerk and manager of the store where the incident occurred. Explain that they did not help you resolve your problem. If your problem is not resolved at this level, it is time to move up to the top.

Take the full name of the district or regional manager and ask for the address, telephone number, or fax number of the corporate headquarters. Also ask for the full name of the CEO. Many times just asking for this information will get you a satisfactory result. If it does not, continue on up the ladder to resolve your problem.

Using telephone, fax or mail, get in touch with the CEO at the corporate headquarters. This should afford you a satisfactory conclusion with your problem. Having to go further in the pursuit of settling your problem is highly unlikely. A major corporation does not want to invest time with or receive negative publicity from a disatisfied customer. Your persistence will have paid off.

Independently Owned Stores

The same procedure is followed here as when dealing with a chain store. You have to keep going until you reach the top "head." In the case of the independently owned store, you must take a different path to reach the top. I will now explain how to attack this problem to get you a satisfactory result.

Start by returning to the establishment and explaining your complaint to the clerk. Remember, *never* lose your temper. Remain calm and keep your voice low. If the clerk does not resolve the problem to your complete satisfaction, you must start your climb to the top. Ask if the store has a manager and see him or her.

Explain your problem to the manager and ask him or her what he or she can do for you. If the response is not satisfactory to you, ask for the owner of the establishment. Ask for the owner's name and how you can get in touch with him or her. If the owner does not normally come into the store, get a telephone number, a fax number, or an address.

Using any of the above methods, get in touch with the owner. Explain your problem to him or her. Tell him or her whom you spoke with and the results from that conversation. If the owner does not give you complete satisfaction, it is time to move forward on to the top.

It is time now to contact the state Department of Consumer Affairs. You can find this agency in your telephone book. Look in the "white pages" under "government listings", or go on Google search. Call and explain your problem. They will investigate your accusations. They must follow through on any complaints referred to them by consumers.

This should be the place where you achieve complete satisfaction. If by any chance you are in the small minority who are not satisfied with the results, you can still continue on to the judicial system.

In order to initiate a lawsuit, you must proceed to the proper court. In this case, it is the small-claims court. This is the easiest court to negotiate. It is a court of the people. You do not need an attorney to use this court. It is the place to recover monetary damages. Each state has a maximum amount you can sue for. More than likely, your claim will fall in this category. Even if you are a little above the maximum, this court will be the easiest to navigate. It will be to your advantage to use it and settle for a little less.

Use the telephone book under "government listings" or use Google search to get the address and, if need be, directions to the courthouse. Go to the courthouse and tell them you want to sue for damages. For a small fee, you can take out a summons and sue the establishment and also the manufacturers of the damaged merchandise. It is always advisable when initiating a lawsuit to sue everyone involved with your complaint. All you have to do is fill out a form and pay a small fee; they will give you a time and date for your court appearance. It is just that simple. The court will notify the establishment and the manufacturer. There is nothing further for you to do at this time.

In the majority of cases, the owner of the establishment and the manufacturer, not wanting to take the time to appear in court, will contact you to negotiate a settlement. If you feel it is a reasonable offer, you can accept it, and your problem is solved. If you do not accept this offer, you have the right to continue on to your "day in court."

When going to court, you must bring documented proof to substantiate your story. Bring the damaged garment and any written correspondence with you. Give the names of everyone you spoke with and their capacity. Bring the receipt you were given when you took the garment to the establishment. Talk slowly and to the point when you relate your story to the judge. You must be extremely polite when speaking to the judge, calling him "Your Honor." When the owner or the manufacturer gives his or her side of the story, stay calm even if you believe what he or she is saying is totally untrue. *Do not* lose your temper. You will be given the opportunity to give your answer to his or her story. The judge will decide your case on the evidence and the true facts. If you are correct, the judge should rule in your favor. If the owner and/or manufacturer will not attend the court session you will win by default.

Using this method and following the steps through to the end, you will be able to recover your loss and also achieve a good sense of accomplishment. You will recover money damages for your damaged merchandise, and your self-esteem will soar. You will feel confident that you can do it alone and succeed.

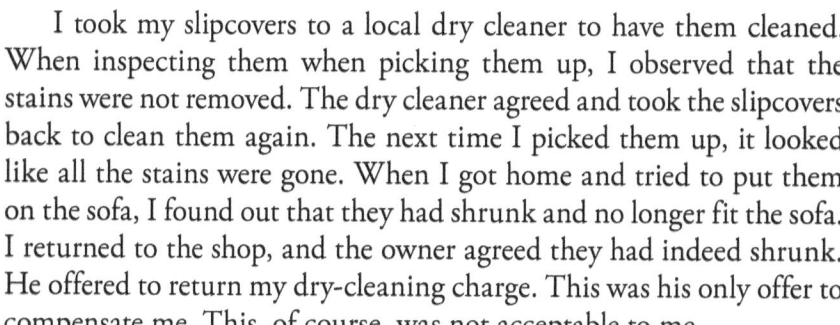

I took my slipcovers to a local dry cleaner to have them cleaned. When inspecting them when picking them up, I observed that the stains were not removed. The dry cleaner agreed and took the slipcovers back to clean them again. The next time I picked them up, it looked like all the stains were gone. When I got home and tried to put them on the sofa, I found out that they had shrunk and no longer fit the sofa. I returned to the shop, and the owner agreed they had indeed shrunk. He offered to return my dry-cleaning charge. This was his only offer to compensate me. This, of course, was not acceptable to me.

I proceeded to small-claims court and took out a summons. I received a court date. A few days before my court appearance was scheduled, I received a call from the owner of the establishment. He made an offer to compensate me, and although it wasn't for the full value of the slipcovers, I decided to accept because I felt it was a good offer since the slipcovers weren't new.

Chapter 5

GOVERNMENT AGENCIES

Now I will discuss how to deal with problems with government agencies. I will explain how to solve these problems quickly and easily. The following is a partial list of where you may run into problems with government agencies:

- motor vehicles
- Internal Revenue Service
- real estate taxes
- public housing
- social services
- city health and hospitals
- Medicare
- Medicaid
- food stamps
- city and state colleges and universities
- unemployment
- vital statistics
- passports
- veterans of the armed services

You will use these agencies all through your life. Whether you are a child, a young adult, or a senior citizen, you must at one time or another deal with government agencies. It doesn't matter if you are rich, middle class, or poor, everyone uses government agencies to deal with these problems at some time during their lives.

Trying to get information from any government agency is usually a frustrating and time-consuming ordeal. Just trying to get some simple information is very difficult. Have you ever tried to get someone on the telephone at a government agency? This could turn out to be a few hours' ordeal, or maybe a few days, or even possibly weeks.

One problem could be trying to find out if you are eligible for a certain government program. Even after obtaining and filing the application, you may never hear whether your application was accepted or not for the program you applied to. You never receive a definitive answer to your request. You are repeatedly told to just keep waiting. They are unable to trace your application or even confirm that it was received.

Occasionally the need to use a specific city or state health facility may arise. This may create a very difficult problem. There may be a highly specialized facility that you may need to use. This facility, although in your state, may be located in another county or city. You are told you are not entitled to use this facility because of its location.

Real estate taxes and water taxes are other areas where problems and disputes arise. The agencies that deal with these taxes are usually very hard to contact. Even when you get through to them, you may still be unable to resolve your problem. It is extremely hard to find the right person who has the ability to solve your particular problem.

Vital statistics, such as records of birth, death, passports, deeds, licenses, titles, and so on are areas where difficulties can arise. Trying to locate needed documents may prove to be extremely difficult to achieve on your own. Just trying to find the proper agency to start your search could prove quite frustrating. Obtaining these documents can be imperative to executing certain tasks.

As you can see, the areas where there may be problems are too numerous to list. So if you have any problems that have to do with government agencies, I will explain to you how to solve them quickly and painlessly. I will instruct you step by step how to achieve a satisfactory conclusion to these situations.

If you know what government agency you want to contact, start with that agency. Call information or use Google search to locate the agency. When you find the department you want, start by calling them up. If you can get through to them in a reasonable length of time, relate your problem to them. When you relate your problem to the agency, occasionally it may be solved at this level. If it is not, do not become discouraged. No matter what you are told at this level as to why you cannot receive what you are requesting, you can go on to achieve a good result.

The next step to solving your problem should be taken if you cannot reach the agency by telephone; you do not know which agency you need to get in touch with; or you did get in touch with the agency, but they were unable to solve your problem to your complete satisfaction.

You must now proceed to your elected officials. Again, call information or go on the Internet (use Google search) and look up your councilman, assemblyman, or senator in your district. It does not matter which party they belong to. They are your district representatives, and you are their constituent. Call the offices of these officials. Tell them you are a constituent and need their help. These people are elected by the public and are there to serve you. This is why they are called public servants.

You can contact them in person at their local headquarters, or if you wish, you can call them up on the telephone. Either way, explain what your problem is and why you need their help. They will tell you what to do next. If you called on the telephone, they may ask you to write a letter explaining your problem. They may ask you to come into the office in person. Your problem may have to be directed to a state or federal official. If so, they will explain to you how to get in touch with him or her. Whatever they ask you to do, you *must follow* their instructions.

After you have turned your problem over to elected officials, there is nothing more you have to do. They will follow your problem through to a conclusion. Once the problem is turned over to them, they will work on it until it is solved. Understandably, they have contacts in all areas of government. When an inquiry comes from a government official, you can be sure they will receive a timely reply. The answer they receive will be sent to you as soon as they receive it. Your problem will be resolved one way or the other, and you will know that this is the final answer.

As you have just read, this is a simple noncomplicated method to follow. The results are absolutely guaranteed. All the stress and frustrations you experienced to get an answer will have been eliminated.

Problems are very different and at the same time very similar for everyone. Your problems are not unique for you; everyone at one time or another experiences similar problems. Remember the Golden Rule of negotiation: *"Go to the head, not to the tail."* Using this rule, you can solve any problem that occurs in your life. I cannot possibly cover every problem that can occur, but using these methods, you will be able to adjust these steps and use them for your individual problems.

Chapter 6

NAVIGATING THE JUDICIAL SYSTEM

The judicial system in the United States of America is designed so that every citizen has the right to use it. Our government has granted us inalienable rights to life, liberty, and the pursuit of happiness. Therefore, no one is denied from using the judicial system because of race, religion, gender, or lack of finances.

To keep our country from becoming a police state, our founding fathers put many safeguards in the judicial system. One such safeguard is found in the criminal justice system. In this country, you are presumed innocent until proven guilty. If you are accused of committing a crime, you are entitled to a trial, and your peers must find you innocent or guilty. Anyone accused of a crime must be represented by an attorney in court. To ensure the poor will receive equal justice with the wealthy, they must have legal representation. If the accused cannot afford to engage an attorney, the state will assign one to him free of charge. This is called a "pro bono" attorney, which means for the (public) good.

Another safeguard to ensure justice for the citizens of this country is to be able to engage an attorney on contingency. This means you do not have to pay the attorney unless you win your case. If you are injured in any way, you can hire an attorney on contingency. Whether you are injured physically, psychologically, or financially, attorneys will work on contingency. You must explain the reason for your lawsuit, and if the attorney feels you were wronged under the law, he may be happy to take the case on contingency

You must sign a contract with the attorney that will define the amount he will take from your money judgment. It will also explain when and how the payment must be made. This amount will be determined as a percentage of whatever you recover for your damages. It will also include the attorney's expenditures that are needed to prove your case in court. These expenditures may include, but are not limited to, specialists who will testify for you, messengers, telephone calls, and traveling expenses incurred to and from meetings and court appearances.

There is still another safeguard to protect those who cannot afford an attorney: you can represent yourself in court without an attorney. This is known as "pro se." This means by yourself, with no attorney. In this country no one is denied their day in court because they cannot afford an attorney. Unfortunately, many people simply are not informed of this situation. It is *not easy* to proceed to court pro se, but armed with the right information, it can be done. First, you must feel absolutely certain you will do what it takes to get a satisfactory conclusion to your problem, but you also must be willing to not achieve the result you desire. Your chances of getting a satisfactory conclusion will be small, but you will always have the satisfaction that you tried. It will be time–consuming, and you must be dedicated to the course you have undertaken. Armed with the information on how to proceed, you will be able to do so.

In the following chapters, I will explain step by step how to navigate the different courts in the judicial system. First, let me list the different courts you can navigate yourself or with an attorney.

- small-claims court
- civil court or superior court
- State Supreme Court
- probate court

Chapter 7

SMALL-CLAIMS COURT

The lowest court is the small-claims court. This court is designed for people to use without an attorney. It is the place to proceed to when you are seeking monetary restitution from any individual, group, or business. This court has a maximum amount you can sue for. In New York, it is $3,000. If the amount you are seeking is slightly above the maximum of this court, because of the ease of going to this court, you might settle for a lesser amount and proceed in small-claims court. It is a fast and simple process going through this court.

First find where the court is located. Call information or go on the Internet. Get the address and go to the courthouse. If you need directions, you should call first, and they will give you directions to the courthouse. Go to the courthouse and explain that you would like to take out a summons to sue someone. For a small fee, they will give you a form to fill out. You will be asked for the name and address of the party you are suing, your name and address, the amount for which you are suing, and the reason for your lawsuit. When you give back this form, you will be given a court date. It is just that simple. The court will notify the defendant as to the time to appear in court. You have nothing more to do but appear in court on your court date.

Arrive at court *on time*. You should have all your proofs, and if applicable, your witnesses. You will be allowed to tell your story to the judge, *but* everything you say must be backed up with written records or witnesses to the facts. Your story alone cannot win your case; it must be substantiated by the written proofs. This is the only way the judge can determine who is right.

If you follow the above steps, you can achieve justice in this court. You will be compensated for the wrong done to you.

Chapter 8

CIVIL COURT OR SUPERIOR COURT

For amounts of monetary restitution that exceed the limits for small-claims court, you can proceed to civil court or superior court. In New York, you can sue for up to $25,000 in civil court. This court is more difficult and requires a lot more time and effort to navigate alone. It is also more costly. An attorney usually represents people who sue in civil court. But it can be done pro se if you cannot afford to retain an attorney. You must be willing to put in the time. If you do, proving your case alone will be very difficult, but the reward is that you will come away with a wonderful feeling of accomplishment knowing you tried and perhaps proved your case.

Get the address of the civil court by calling information or using the Internet. Go to the courthouse and explain that you are there "pro se" and you want to take out a summons to sue for monetary damages. Explain that you cannot afford to retain an attorney and that you want to use this court yourself. They will explain how to proceed. There will be a charge to file a summons. Fill out all the forms carefully. In civil court you will be responsible to notify the defendant regarding your lawsuit. You will be given forms with which to serve him and instructed as to how this must be accomplished. Follow the instructions that are given to you. You will be pleasantly surprised to see how capable you are of proceeding through civil court alone. When you return the proof that the defendant was served, they will notify you as to the date of your trial.

Appear in court *on time*. Be sure to have all your documented proofs with you. Remember, everything you say *must* be documented with written proof. Before arriving in court, you must have a paper trail. Everything you did prior to arriving at court must be documented.

When you are called before the judge, he most likely will inquire about the fact that an attorney does not represent you. You will reply, "I'm here pro se because I cannot afford to retain an attorney." The judge will be very patient with you. It is his duty to be sure you understand the proceedings to ensure you are given a fair trial. Be *extremely polite*. Do not lose your temper no matter what the defendant says about you. Refer to the judge as "Your Honor." Ask permission before you reply to accusations or wish to say something, for example, "May I speak Your Honor". It is the judge's duty to give you all the time you need to prove your case. A court stenographer will be taking the minutes of your trial. The judge knows that you can appeal his decision on the grounds that you did not understand the proceedings. This is why you will be pleasantly surprised to see how patiently everything will be explained to you.

If you are right under the law, the judge will decide in your favor. You will have received restitution for the injustice against you. The fact that you could not afford to retain an attorney did not prevent you from seeking justice in our judicial system. You will have accomplished it alone. This fact will make you feel very proud. Whether or not you recovered your loss, you will have sought restitution yourself.

Chapter 9

THE SUPREME COURT

The Supreme Court is the most difficult court to navigate by alone. The most common reasons for being in the State Supreme Court are for personal injury, malpractice, and divorce. For malpractice and personal injury, you will be able to retain a contingency attorney. For these types of lawsuits, there is no need to go to court pro se. Divorce is one instance when under certain conditions you may need to go to the State Supreme Court pro se. Remember, only if you truly do not have the funds to retain a competent attorney should you precede pro se. A favorable result cannot be guaranteed.

In the State Supreme Court you can only proceed by submitting written documents. These are known as petitions to the court in the form of a motion. A petition or motion tells the court why you came to the court and what relief you are seeking from them. You cannot ask for help verbally in the Supreme Court. Your plea for help must be submitted in the form of a written document. You must be able to use a computer word processor or a typewriter to prepare these written documents. If you cannot do this, you cannot navigate the State Supreme Court.

You can use your computer and go online to find any form you will need to get into the State Supreme Court. Use the search engine and look up "legal forms." Pick the form that corresponds with your problem. If you do not have a computer or cannot negotiate the Internet, you can get these forms from a good stationery store. You can find such stores next to all courthouses, or you can look them up in the yellow pages of your telephone book. You will be able to look up the form number from a directory book by looking up the problem that you want to solve. In this way, you will be able to purchase the correct form.

The next step you must follow is to take your form to the courthouse. Ask information to direct you to the courthouse library. Here you can look up a book containing the type of petition you want to submit to the court. You can use this as a guide for filling out your petition. The most important part of writing a petition is that you must use the *proper form*. Each line must be in the proper place. Follow the example from the petition that you have found in the library. Write everything in its place. Also, *never* abbreviate any words when writing your petition. Every word must be written in full on legal documents.

After you have written your petition, you are now ready to submit it to the State Supreme Court. You must make at least four copies of your document. Go to the courthouse and tell them you want to submit a petition. You will be directed to an office where you will have to purchase an "index" number to put on your petition. You can only pay for this service with cash if you are not an attorney. You can call ahead to find the cost of this index number. It is a minimal amount, but it must be paid in cash. Once you write the index number on your petition, you are ready to submit it to the "motion office." When you submit your petition to the clerk, he or she will look it over to see if it was written correctly. If it is correct, he or she will accept it. If it is not correct, he or she will tell you how to correct it.

If you are answering an action against you, your work is finished. If you are bringing an action against another party after summitting it and having it accepted you must serve the other party with a copy of your petition so the other party can answer you when you get in front of the judge. You must have the proof of service with you when you resubmit your petition. Without the proof of service, your petition will not be accepted. The petition must be served in person by anyone not connected to the case that is above the age of twenty-one, or a paid process server.

After your petition and proof of service is accepted, you will be notified as to the date of your appearance in court. Arrive on time on this date with a copy of your petition. Take a seat and wait for your name to be called by the court clerk. When you are called, you will be directed to stand before the judge on either the "petitioner's" or the "respondent's" side. The judge will ask you, "Do you have an attorney?" You will respond, "I am here pro se."

The judge will be very patient with you because you have no attorney. He or she must be certain you understand what is happening and give you ample time to explain your side of the dispute. The court stenographer will be taking the minutes of the proceeding, and if you do not understand what's going on, the judge's decision can be appealed.

The judge will ask you a few questions, but he or she will have already read your petition and the respondent's petition. He or she will only want to clarify some facts written in the petitions. When all the facts are stated, your court appearance will be over. You will be notified of the judge's decision by mail a few weeks later.

When you receive your decision, you will have navigated the Supreme Court by yourself. You must be prepared for the decision, favorable or not, since going to court alone without counsel is a risk. No matter what the decision might be, you will be proud of yourself that you were not denied your day in court because you could not afford to retain an attorney.

Chapter 10

PROBATE COURT

Probate court is where your last will and testament is probated and the final accounting is filed. In New York, this court is known as the Surrogate's Court. When a person passes away leaving a will, an attorney will probate it. The executor must distribute the estate to the heirs. Inheritance taxes, if applicable, must be paid. All expenses and debts must also be paid. After all this is taken care of, the final accounting is filed in probate court. This is to assure that the last wishes of the deceased are carried out properly and all debts and taxes are paid.

Problems occur during probate when the heirs feel the deceased's wishes are not being followed correctly or if the executor does not perform his or her duties in a timely manner. If the heirs' concerns are not answered to their satisfaction, they can go to probate court. If you cannot afford to retain an attorney, you can take your copy of the will and go to probate court yourself.

Get the address of the courthouse from information or the Internet, and with your copy of the will, go down to the courthouse. Explain that you came to the court because you wanted to know why you hadn't received your legacy. You will be given some forms to fill out, including an "Affidavit of Service."

Return home and complete the forms given to you. The forms are self-explanatory. Simply insert the names needed to start an action in court. There will be a place to insert the name of the executor and his or her address. Make several copies of this form. One copy must be served on the executor. Anyone twenty-one years of age and not connected to the proceeding can serve these papers, or you can pay a process server. The person who serves the papers on the executor will then fill out the "Affidavit of Service." When this process is complete, go back to the courthouse with your papers and submit them to the court. You will be notified as to a date for your court appearance.

Arrive at the courthouse on time. Go to the courtroom you are assigned to. Wait for your name to be called. You will be told to approach the bench. The executor will most likely not appear in person. The attorney who works for him or her and who is probating the will most likely will be present in court. The judge will allow you to explain your grievance. The attorney will be allowed to answer your accusations. If you have a legitimate complaint, the judge will decide the issue in your favor. If it was merely a lack of communication and there were no improprieties on the part of the executor and the attorney, at least the judge will explain to you what is happening. You will feel assured that the last wishes of the deceased are being carried out correctly.

Chapter 11

CONCLUSION

Having read my book, you now posses the knowledge you need to help you solve your merchandise and service problems, as well as, if needed, how to navigate the judicial system. Life is complicated; being able to make it a little easier is a well-deserved commodity. When you can solve a problem quickly and easily, you can eliminate much unnecessary stress. You can live your life much more peacefully. There is more time to enjoy life's pleasures with friends and family. Gaining more free stressless time is a bonus we can all appreciate. Unfortunately, problems are unavoidable and something we must all experience. Being able to solve them quickly and painlessly is a gift we will all enjoy.

When you are faced with disputes concerning merchandise and service issues, you now possess the knowledge to bring them to a satisfactory conclusion. My methods are not complicated and can be applied to many different situations. Basically, by following the instructions in my book, you will be able to recover from your financial mishaps. Using my easy-to-apply steps, you can recover your losses.

Many times individuals feel it is futile to try to gain compensation from a large corporation or even a small business owner. You have to overcome the conception that one lone person cannot possibly succeed against corporations. As you have read, this is certainly not true. Almost every situation can be brought to a satisfactory conclusion when you possess the proper information on how to proceed. Fear of failing is eliminated with knowledge, and you will be able to proceed in a wide variety of situations. Your self-esteem will soar with every successful result.

Some people go through their entire lives without ever having to use the judicial system. Others unfortunately find themselves needing to use this system. Having the knowledge of how to proceed eliminates much of the anxiety.

After reading my book, you are now knowledgeable about our judicial system and how it works. Knowing which court handles your specific problem is very helpful in finding justice for yourself. You can find the proper court to go to for the different problems you may face. Knowing where to go and whether to retain an attorney or go there alone is a very useful tool. You now know which court and which attorney you should use in the judicial system, as well as how to represent yourself in court. You know which method of payment to use for your attorney. In other words, would you be paying him or her a retainer upfront or on a contingency basis, or can you retain him or her pro bono? You can now decide if in certain situations you possess the ability and dedication to go to court by yourself without an attorney.

If you decide to use the judicial system on your own, you must realize you are not a professional attorney. You have no formal education in the field of law, nor have you passed a bar exam. Only in very extreme situations should you proceed to court on your own pro se. You must be willing to put in a lot of time and effort, and also be willing to accept defeat. Using this knowledge, you now know that you will never be turned away from going to court, and you will have the satisfaction of being able to have tried.

Each court has its own level of difficulties. The easiest court to negotiate is small-claims court. Most people come to this court without an attorney. As you have read, it only entails knowing the maximum dollar amount of compensation you can receive and the location of the courthouse.

Civil court is for dollar amounts that exceed small-claims court. You can negotiate it alone without an attorney, but only when retaining one is monetarily impossible. The choice is yours alone. Be willing to fail, but try your best to succeed. Be aware that it requires time and commitment to proceed alone. If going alone is your only option, you now know how to accomplish this. By all means, go for it. You have nothing to lose. Not trying will result in the same financial loss. The decision is yours, and now you have the knowledge to proceed alone.

Probate court is not very difficult to proceed by yourself. You must be a recipient in the will, either a beneficiary or been left a legacy. Your complaint must be substantiated to the court. Some examples are how the executors are handling the distribution, or perhaps problems with the will itself. The process is easily accomplished following the steps outlined in the corresponding chapter. You can always proceed with the help of an attorney, but now you have the knowledge to proceed alone.

As you have read, going to the Supreme Court by yourself, pro se, is extremely difficult. You must first find the correct forms and then be able to use a word possessor, write motions, and submit them to the court. Unless you are a detail-oriented person and have time to dedicate many hours of work, you should not attempt going to court pro se.

This is an educational book written to help consumers handle life's problems. After your first attempt using my instructions and achieving a satisfactory conclusion, you will be pleasantly surprised how easy it was. You will not hesitate to apply these methods for all your problems. With every successful result, your self-esteem will soar. Not only will you achieve financial success, but you will become a more confident human being. It will make you unafraid to deal with all of life's challenges.

I have been very successful using these methods. You can also achieve success. I cannot guarantee the same results I enjoyed, but I feel confident that you will achieve success too. If you follow my Golden Rule of negotiation by going to the head, not the tail, going up the ladder one step at a time, you can come away successful. Good luck and remember: *You can do it alone.*

www.ingramcontent.com/pod-product-compliance
Lightning Source LLC
Chambersburg PA
CBHW021038180526
45163CB00005B/2174